Copyright © 2012 by: 3 Legged Dog Publishing LLC
All rights reserved.

ISBN: 0-9885169-1-8
ISBN-13: 978-0-9885169-1-5

This book is dedicated to those who have adopted or are thinking of adopting a pet to complete the family circle. Take care of these little creatures and give them unconditional love. They come with open paws and will do anything to please you. All they ask in return is a safe and "Forever Home" to live out their remaining days in joy and happiness at your side.

A very special thank you to Alan, without his great encouragement this book would still be in my "I think I'll work on this later" folder.

I Dream

Rambler's Adoption Journey

Written by Julie Jones and Illustrated by Toni Pawlowsky.

THE CAR

I dream of a shiny car.
The lights are bright and it sees me.
I cannot run.
I'm falling down.
Mommy and daddy are you there?

THE BRIGHT ROOM

I dream of a bright white room.
I see many shapes and a small light in the corner.
I'm cold and very sleepy.
I think I see my dad.
He whispers, "Close your eyes little one".

THE COZY BED

I dream of a soft and cozy bed.
I try to move…my leg feels funny.
I see my dad sitting down.
He says, "Sleep now, you're ok".
I look up at him…I feel safe.

THE BIG YARD

I dream of a big green grassy back yard.

I want to run and jump.

I fall and try to get up.

Why am I falling?

I see my mom and dad…they are far away.

THE NOISY BIRD

I dream of a large black bird.
The bird is chirping and squawking.
I take a small hop.
I look down at my three legs.
I see the bird…it looks at me and winks.

THE COLD NIGHT

I dream of a cold and windy night.

I'm hungry and my tummy hurts.

I'm scared and look for a warm place to rest.

I snuggle up to a big old tree.

Why am I alone?

THE SUNNY DAY

I dream of a bright sunny day.
I'm sleepy and very thirsty.
I hop to a big hole with water.
I see a man waiting for me.

THE BEACH

I dream of a sandy and warm beach.
I 'm not hungry or cold.
I have friends to play with.
I have a warm bed to sleep in.
I think I have a new home…Can I stay?

THE NEW CAR

I dream of a car sitting on the beach.
I see a new lady and man.
I am shaking and fall down.
I get up and see another one like me.
Are you my new friend?

THE RIDE

I dream of a ride down a winding road.
I have my face in the wind.
I am happy and my new friend is happy.
I want to run and jump.
Am I going home?

THE BIG HOUSE

I dream of a big brown house.
I stand on the grass and see the door open.
I run in and look around.
I jump into a small bed.
I hope this is mine…Can I stay here?

THE DREAM BEGINS

I dream of big green yard
with a noisy bird and lots of water.
I hear a call, "Come here, Rambler".
I look at them and take a small step…I'm afraid.
I see my dad walking towards me…
he hugs me and smiles.
I now have a forever home…
I close my eyes and sleep.

www.ingramcontent.com/pod-product-compliance
Lightning Source LLC
Chambersburg PA
CBHW041542040426
42446CB00002B/195